||| || ||||| || | ||| ||||||||||| ||| |||

W9-AOW-410

white wine

discovering, exploring, enjoying

RYLAND
PETERS
& SMALL
London New York

Jonathan Ray

photography by Alan Williams

white wine

discovering, exploring, enjoying

For Vickie, with love

Designer Sarah Rock

Senior editor Henrietta Heald

Production manager Patricia Harrington

Art director Leslie Harrington

Publishing director Alison Starling

First published in 2001
This edition published in 2008
in the UK by Ryland Peters & Small
20-21 Jockey's Fields
London WC1R 4BW and
in the USA by Ryland Peters & Small Inc.
519 Broadway, 5th Floor
New York, NY 10012
www.rylandpeters.com
10 9 8 7 6 5 4 3 2 1

ISBN: 978-1-84597-735-1

A CIP record for this book is available
from the British Library and from the
Library of Congress.

Printed in China.

Contents

Introduction

White wines can be bone dry or richly sweet; they can be headily alcoholic or light and refreshing; and they can be still or sparkling. To complicate matters further, more wine than ever befor is being produced, and in many more countries, so it is little wonder that some of us feel overwhelmed by the endless rows of bottles in the supermarket.

Resist the urge to panic; instead, take a deep breath and simply start at the beginning. Climate, soil and methods of production all make significant contributions to the way a wine tastes, but the most important factor is the grape itself, so a few hours spent differentiating between Sauvignon Blanc and Chardonnay, Riesling and Sémillon will be time well spent. Once you can identify the different grape varieties and the wines that they make, you will discover the wines you like and the wines you don't, and you will be well on your way to becoming an expert. Further research - which, let's be frank, will require some dedicated sluicing and slurping - will help you to determine which wines make the ideal partners for particular foods.

bottle shapes and sizes

In this age of designer chic, European wine producers are less strict than they were about using the traditional bottles of their respective regions; while producers from the New World are divided between those who use the shapes most associated with each particular variety and those who bottle their wines in whatever shape pleases them. Nevertheless, the shape and colour of a wine bottle remain useful tools for identifying the style and type of wine inside.

As a rule, the sweet and dry white wines of Bordeaux along with New World Sauvignon Blancs and Semillons come in high-shouldered bottles of green or clear glass; white burgundies, Chablis, white Rhônes and many New World Chardonnays are in green bottles with sloping shoulders; while the aromatic wines of Alsace, Germany and beyond come in tall, slender bottles. Those from Alsace are green, whereas German wines have

a further distinction, in that wines from the Mosel (known as Moselles) come in green bottles and those from the Rhine (known as Hocks) come in brown bottles.

Apart from two rare exceptions, champagne and sparkling wines come in dark green bottles with sloping shoulders and a pronounced indentation in the base called a punt. Champagne producers are famous for using outsized bottles for their wines, without which no grand celebration is complete. Sizes range from a quarter-bottle to a nebuchadnezzar.

Quarter-bottle = 18.75cl
Half-bottle = 37.5cl
Bottle = 75cl
Magnum = 2 bottles
Double magnum = 4 bottles
Jeroboam = 4 bottles
Rehoboam = 6 bottles
Methuselah = 8 bottles
Salmanazar = 12 bottles
Balthazar = 16 bottles
Nebuchadnezzar = 20 bottles

labels explained

Among the items of information that must, by law, appear on a label on the front or back of a bottle are:

- the wine's name
- the size of the bottle
- the vintage (if there is one)
- the wine's alcoholic strength
- the producer's name and address
- the name of the bottler (if different from the producer)
- the name of the importer
- the name of the shipper (if different from the importer)
- the wine's quality level
- whether the wine contains sulphites
- where the wine was bottled
- the wine's country of origin
- the wine's region and appellation (if relevant)

Some labels also include the grape variety.

Wine labels are there to inform, and if read correctly will tell you all you need to know about the wine itself. Most countries now insist on displaying a government health warning about the hazards of drinking wine (with not a word about the proven benefits). Wines sold in the USA, for example, must show stern admonitions about the perils of alcohol from the Surgeon General, while those sold in France caution pregant women not to drink.

The white wines with the most perplexing labels are those from Germany, and not only because they are often written in indecipherable Gothic script. Information on these labels includes the following terms for the six categories of ripeness.

Kabinett = the driest level of quality wine.

Spätlese = wines made from late-picked grapes.

Auslese = wines made from selected bunches of very ripe grapes.

Trockenbeerenauslese = wines made from dried grapes or those attacked by 'noble rot'.

Beerenauslese = wines made from individually selected grapes.

Eiswein = wines made from grapes picked when frozen, which concentrates the sugar in the juice.

These terms can be linked to levels of sweetness, from Kabinett, the most dry, to the incredibly honeyed Trockenbeerenauslese and intensely sweet Eiswein.

Wine labels are there to help you, and if read correctly

will tell you **everything** you need to know about the wine itself.

single varietals and blends

A single varietal is a wine made wholly, or almost wholly, from a single type of grape – Chardonnay, perhaps, Sauvignon Blanc or Sylvaner. Rules about varietals differ from region to region. For example, in Australia 80 per cent of the wine must come from the named variety, while in the USA it is 75 per cent.

In Europe the tradition is to name the wines after the region of origin rather than after the variety, Alsace being a notable exception. Therefore, if you know you like single-varietal Chardonnays from California or Australia, say, it is helpful to know that all white burgundies, such as Pouilly-Fuissé, Puligny-Montrachet or Meursault, are also single varietals, being 100 per cent Chardonnay.

The art of blending is to marry the wines of two or more varieties together to make a wine greater than the sum of its parts. The process can also encompass different vintages, as in the case of non-vintage champagnes or standard 'house white' burgundies that are blended in such a way as to ensure that they always taste the same.

The blending of different varieties occurs less often in white wines than it does in red wines. In France, for example, the great wines of the Loire, Sancerre and Pouilly Fumé, are 100 per cent Sauvignon Blanc, while white burgundies and Chablis are 100 per cent Chardonnay. Champagne is usually a blend of three varieties, but producers do also make champagnes from both Chardonnay and Pinot Noir on their own.

Some blends are seen only in the New World; in Australia, Semillon/Chardonnay blends are common, but this is an example of a combination that would be prohibited by the restrictive wine laws in most areas of France.

There are strong arguments in favour of blends and of single varietals – arguments that are revisited whenever two or more winemakers are gathered together. Neither style is better than the other. They are simply different, and just because you like the subtlety of one particular blend it does not mean that you won't also appreciate the purity of a particular single varietal.

The art of blending is to marry the wines of two or more varieties together to make a wine greater than the sum of its parts.

chardonnay

Chardonnay is without doubt the world's most popular grape variety. Purists might argue that Riesling makes the finer and more elegant wine, but that view is not reflected in public opinion. Chardonnay is easy to grow, has good acid levels, high alcohol, ages well, blends well with other varieties – and winemakers and wine drinkers can't get enough of it. Since it is difficult to make a poor wine from the grape, it is rare to find a bad Chardonnay.

Chardonnay is responsible for champagne and Chablis, and for such well-known white burgundies as Puligny-Montrachet, Meursault, Corton-Charlemagne and Pouilly-Fuissé. The taste of Chardonnays varies according to where they are grown, on account of variations in climate and wine-makers' techniques. For example, Chardonnays from Burgundy tend to be elegant and lean compared to the big, blousy wines from Australia or

Forget the red wine for once and drink a big oak-aged Chardonnay from Burgundy or Australia with a hearty meat casserole or roast veal, or a Chablis with cheeses such as Brie and Camembert.

California, where warmer climates result in riper grapes. But even in two neighbouring areas there can be pronounced differences, for while white burgundies can be nutty or toasty the wines of Chablis can be steely and flinty.

Chardonnay does spectacularly well in Australia, New Zealand, South Africa, South America, Italy and Spain. It is especially loved by Californians, in whose state it is the most planted grape variety. In fact, to many Americans, the word Chardonnay is synonymous with white wine, so ubiquitous is the variety. But despite these major successes elsewhere, Burgundy remains its spiritual home.

One cannot speak of Chardonnay without also referring to oak, with which it has a special relationship. Oak barrels draw out Chardonnay's best characteristics and give the wine aromas of vanilla, toast and nuts. Oaked and unoaked Chardonnays can be very different; try both.

There are many different types of Riesling with different names which can be confusing. In California the true Riesling is called Johannisberg Riesling; in Australia it is known as Rhine Riesling; and in South Africa as Weisser Riesling.

riesling

True Riesling is the most elegant of grapes and is most at home in Germany, where all the top wines, be they sweet or dry, are Rieslings. The sweet wines are usually affected by noble rot and range in sweetness through Auslese and Beerenauslese to Trockenbeerenauslese.

German Rieslings are frequently light in alcohol and age remarkably well, gaining rich honey flavours as they do so. The grape should be instantly identifiable in the glass, marked out by its distinctive aromas of petrol, peaches, melons, apples and limes.

Remarkably - considering that it is regarded as one of the world's finest grapes, if not the finest - you won't find Riesling in France, other than in Alsace. There, it is considered top dog and makes fresh, lively wines, which, while delicate, are fuller and higher in alcohol than those from neighbouring Germany.

The grape is also widely grown in Austria, making dry, concentrated wines, and in Italy's Friuli and Alto Adige, where it makes light, elegant and aromatic wines.

Riesling is grown in Marlborough, New Zealand, producing wines of excellent acidity and delicacy, and it also features in Argentina and Chile. Most of California is too warm to produce dry Riesling - the drinking public seems only to want Chardonnay anyway - but both Washington State and Ontario in Canada exploit the grape's preference for cool conditions to make wines of great delicacy. Superb examples can be found in Australia in the Barossa, Eden and Clare Valleys.

Drier German Rieslings go well with Pacific Rim cooking and other spicy food, while the sweet ones are perfect with fruit, nuts or puddings.

sauvignon blanc

Sauvignon Blanc is one of the world's major grape varieties, celebrated as much for its distinctive, steely-dry single varietals as it is for its role in the world's finest dessert wines.

France's most celebrated Sauvignon Blancs are Sancerre and Pouilly Fumé from the Loire, where producers don't believe in blending the variety, which is sometimes called Blanc Fumé. They prefer to make single varietals that are fermented and aged in stainless-steel vats rather than in oak, creating wines that are crisp and clean-flavoured with a smoky, mineral quality. Other, lesser-known but good-value Loire wines made from Sauvignon Blanc include Ménétou-Salon, Quincy, Reuilly and Sauvignon de Touraine.

Sauvignon Blanc is more acidic than Chardonnay; to some, this crispness is preferable to the soft butteriness of Chardonnay. The grape is notable for its aromas of freshly cut grass, blackcurrant leaves, gooseberries, asparagus and – remarkably, but undeniably – cat's pee. Some people would argue that, impressive as

Sauvignon Blanc is on its own, it is only when combined with Sémillon that it achieves true greatness. In Bordeaux the dry wines of Entre-Deux-Mers and Graves are blends of Sauvignon Blanc and Sémillon (usually aged in oak), as are the great dessert wines of Barsac and Sauternes and the lesser ones of Ste-Croix du Mont and Monbazillac.

New Zealand produces some stunning Sauvignon Blancs, giving the wines of Sancerre and Pouilly Fumé a very close run for their money. In California, too, Sauvignon Blanc flourishes, thanks to Robert Mondavi, who pioneered the variety in North America, originally calling it Fumé Blanc. Now second in popularity to Chardonnay in the USA, Sauvignon Blanc produces wines that tend to be less grassy than those of New Zealand or the Loire. The grape is also a great success both in Chile and South Africa.

Apart from the sweet wines and fuller dry wines of Bordeaux, most Sauvignon Blancs are best drunk while they are still young – that is, within three or four years of the vintage.

Being light, crisp and refreshing, Sauvignon Blancs make excellent aperitifs as well as enhancing most poultry and fish dishes.

Single-varietal Sémillon goes well with smoked fish, such as trout, haddock or mackerel.

sémillon

Sémillon makes deep-yellow wines that are full-bodied, high in both alcohol and aroma, low in acid, and which age extremely well, being particularly well suited to oak. Sémillon is one of the great unsung grapes of the world, and many people consume it without having heard of it, most notably in the wines of Bordeaux, where Sémillon adds structure to the dry wines of the Graves and the sweet ones of Sauternes and Barsac. It has become more prominent recently thanks to its role in blended wines from the New World, most of which are labelled varietally.

Unblended, Sémillon is apt to make undistinguished, forgettable wines, but when it is combined with Sauvignon Blanc, great things happen. Sauvignon Blanc provides the acidity and aromas, while Sémillon softens Sauvignon Blanc's rougher edges to make sublime wines that are often greater than either variety can make on its own.

Sémillon is susceptible to noble rot and provides the lion's share of the blends that go to make up the finest Sauternes and Barsacs, whose rich, intensely honeyed and utterly delicious wines usually include about 80 per cent Sémillon, 20 per cent Sauvignon Blanc and a slurp of Muscadelle.

Australia – where Semillon has a non-accented 'e' and is sometimes called Hunter Valley Riesling – makes some fine single varietals, mainly in New South Wales and the Hunter Valley, perhaps proving to the doubters that the grape can stand alone. It is also blended very successfully with Chardonnay and makes fine dessert wines. Single-varietal Sémillons are also made in South Africa, mainly in Paarl, Wellington and Franschhoek Valleys, and in Chile, where it provides two-thirds of all white wine produced, much of it pretty basic – the grape tending to be fat and oily – and little of which is exported.

Chenin Blanc is an **extraordinary grape** in that it can produce still and **sparkling wine, sweet and dry wine**, fortified wine and spirits.

chenin blanc

The Chenin Blanc grape comes originally from the Loire Valley in France, where it is often known as Pineau de la Loire, and where its versatility is much in evidence. It is there that it produces such wines as the dry Savennières from Anjou, the dry, the sparkling or the utterly delicious sweet Vouvrays from Touraine, the late-harvest Côteaux du Layons and the sparkling wines of Saumur.

Thousands of litres of indifferent and sharp table wine are made from Chenin Blanc in the Loire too, indicating that it is not at its best when made into a dry wine.

Its susceptibility to botrytis, the noble rot that concentrates the sugar in the grape, makes Chenin Blanc ideal for producing dessert wines, the best of which can last for decades, gaining beautiful golden hues and rich honey flavours as they age. Its high natural acidity is perfect for making sparkling wine and it is an important component in the blend responsible for the world's oldest sparkling wine, Blanquette de Limoux from the Midi.

Chenin Blanc seems to do best in marginal climates and it is grown successfully in New Zealand and in South Africa, where, once known as Steen, it is the country's most popular variety, making increasingly delicious wines.

Elsewhere in the New World, Chenin Blanc is rarely accorded the respect that it receives in the Loire or South Africa. In Australia it is used mainly for blending into commercial wines, while in California the clamour for Chardonnay and Sauvignon Blanc means that there is currently little consumer interest in it.

Nothing goes better with strawberries and cream or a fruit tart than a sweet Vouvray.

Gewurztraminer goes well with strong cheeses and spicy food such as Thai or Chinese cuisine, as well as with smoked salmon and Pacific Rim cooking.

Gewurztraminer may be the most difficult variety to spell and to pronounce (it is generally spelt without an umlaut), but its deep golden colour and exotic and heady aromas of lychees, spice, flowers, peaches and apricots are unforgettable, making it a cinch to spot at blind tastings.

Although it is grown throughout Europe and is supposed to have originated in Italy's Alto Adige (where it is still known as Traminer Aromatico), Gewurztraminer is most at home in Alsace. Here the variety is at its most pungent, making sweet-smelling but intensely dry wines, high in alcohol, low in acidity and bursting with spicy flavours. In great years, rich and honeyed late-harvest wines, known as *vendanges tardives*, are made, as too, in exceptional years, are botrytis-affected wines known as *séléction de grains nobles*.

Gewürz is the German word for spice, and Gewurztraminer is highly regarded both in Germany, especially in Rheinpfalz just over the border from Alsace, and in Austria. The grape does best in cool climates, and in the New World it is happiest in New Zealand, although there are some plantings in Australia too. In California it is grown only in the cooler areas such as Carneros, Anderson Valley, Monterey County and Mendocino, where it makes scented wines, noticeably softer and less spicy than those of Alsace. Some wines are also being made successfully in Oregon in America's Pacific north-west.

gewurztraminer

marsanne

Marsanne is a vigorous grape that produces deep-coloured, brown-tinged wine high in alcohol with a distinctive and heady aroma reminiscent of apples, pears, glue, nuts, spice and almonds.

The grape's full flavour, coupled with a low acidity, means that it is ideal for blending; the variety with which it is inextricably linked is Roussanne. It is a highly successful partnership, responsible for such white wines of the northern Rhône as Côtes du Rhône Blanc, Crozes–Hermitage, Hermitage and St-Joseph. Marsanne is also one of the grapes permitted in the blend that makes the southern Rhône's comparatively rare white Châteauneuf-du-Pape.

Although Marsanne is traditionally seen as making long-lived, full-bodied wines that can sometimes be dull when young, modern winemaking techniques are changing such perceptions, and fruity, perfumed wines are being produced for early consumption. When

A fine white Rhône is perfect with heavily sauced lobster or crab or with fish dishes such as grilled tuna or turbot.

young, its wines are now flowery and aromatic; when old, they are rich and nutty; indeed, it seems nowadays that only in its middle age is it dull. Increasingly grown in the Midi, Marsanne makes fleshy white wines in Cassis, and the dry, sweet, still and sparkling wines of St-Péray, south of Cornas in the northern Rhône. It is a permitted ingredient in the northern Rhône's Syrah-dominated red Hermitage, and is grown successfully in the Valais, in Switzerland, where it is known as Ermitage Blanc.

As for the New World, Marsanne has been grown in Victoria in Australia since the 1860s, making big, long-lived wines, but it is seen only occasionally in California, where it appears as either single varietals or blended with its old Rhône friend Roussanne.

pinot blanc

Found in almost every wine region in the world,
Pinot Blanc is best known in Alsace (where, unusually
for a French wine region, it is sold under its varietal name)
and in Italy, where it is an important part of
the blend that makes Soave.

Pinot Blanc is not dissimilar to Chardonnay, to which it was once thought to be related, although it is not nearly so flavoursome, complex or sophisticated. At its best it should be fresh, lively and appealing with flavours of yeast and apples backed up by the faintest hints of honey. But although it is invariably light and pleasing on the palate, it never really seems to have a great deal to say. Its high acidity makes it ideal for making sparkling wines and it is used as the base for most of Alsace's fizzy Crémant d'Alsace.

In Alsace, Pinot Blanc also makes drinkable, if undramatic, dry white wines, the lightest of the region which, while well regarded, are usually eclipsed by those of Pinot Gris. Modest amounts are also grown in Burgundy, usually for blending with Chardonnay into the region's basic white wine – Bourgogne Blanc. It is grown all over Italy – where it is called Pinot Bianco – notably in the Veneto, Alto Adige and Lombardy, where it makes pleasant sparkling wine.

Alsace Pinot Blanc goes especially well with fish pâtés,
light salads and pasta with seafood sauces.

As Weissburgunder, Pinot Blanc is increasingly popular in Germany, making both dry and sweet wines - especially in Baden and Rheinpfalz - and it is grown throughout Austria, even being used to make botrytized Trockenbeerenauslese.

Pinot Blanc is ignored by much of the New World. Some is grown in Chile, and a few producers grow it successfully in California; confusingly, much of what is called Pinot Blanc in California is in fact Melon de Bourgogne.

Pinot Gris is low in acid and goes especially well with food; those from Alsace in particular are marvellous with that region's choucroute and cheeses, as well as with cold meats and hot or cold lobster.

pinot gris

Pinot Gris produces fragrant white wines of depth and substance, with styles ranging from crisp, light and dry, to rich, full and honeyed. At its best, it makes a fine alternative to white burgundy and can be full-bodied enough to drink with dishes that are more usually accompanied by red wines. Although technically a white grape, Pinot Gris is a mutation of the red Pinot Noir and it can produce wines that are almost rosé in colour.

Pinot Gris thrives in Alsace (where it is sometimes still known as Tokay d'Alsace or Tokay Pinot-Gris), producing not only big, smoky, dry wines but also the remarkably intense *vendanges tardives*. Around Touraine, in the Loire, it makes charming rosés, and in Valais in Switzerland it results in rich, full wines. While Pinot Gris is oily and fat in Alsace, it is lighter, spritzier and more acidic in Italy, where – known as Pinot

Grigio – it is grown mainly in Friuli, Lombardy and in small areas of Emilia-Romagna.

Germany grows more Pinot Gris (known there as Rulander) than any other country, making juicy wines of low acidity and spicy aroma, especially in Baden, Württemberg and Rheinpfalz.

It is catching on in the New World, growing in popularity in New Zealand California, especially among those bored by the ubiquity of Chardonnay, and there are some plantings of Pinot Gris in Mexico and Willamette Valley in Oregon.

roussanne

Roussanne is the more refined half of the vinous double act it performs with Marsanne. In the northern Rhône, in particular, the two grapes are inextricably linked, joining forces to produce the white versions of Hermitage, Crozes–Hermitage and St-Joseph, as well as being used in small quantities in the red Hermitage blend, adding softness to the otherwise unblended Syrah.

Roussanne is less widely grown than Marsanne, not least because it is prone to powdery mildew and rot and has an irregular yield, but it is the more stylish and polished of the two, and its wines age more gracefully. In the southern Rhône it is used in the blends that make both the red and the white Châteauneuf-du-Pape.

Roussanne is also grown in Languedoc–Roussillon, where the warm climate ensures that its tendency to ripen late is less of a problem than it is in the northern Rhône, or in Savoie in eastern France, where small amounts of single-varietal Roussanne can be found if you look hard enough.

Roussanne has a spicier flavour than Marsanne, and while its wines are delicious when young, with a tendency to blossom in later years, they can, like those of Marsanne, be a bit grumpy in middle age. The two grapes also combine to make the Rhône's *méthode traditionelle* wine, St-Péray, a full-flavoured sparkler with an almost nutty taste.

White Rhônes go well with smoked eel, smoked salmon and gravadlax.

viognier

Viognier has now become extremely fashionable among growers and drinkers alike, having gained its reputation by producing the extraordinarily intense dry white wines from the tiny vineyards of Château Grillet and Condrieu next door to Côte Rôtie in the northern Rhône. Restaurants that had never heard of Viognier ten years ago are now stocking several examples of the variety, which are well worth seeking out, although they are likely to be expensive.

Good Viogniers are big-boned beauties with alluring, but fleeting, scents of peaches and apricots, comparable in their headiness of aroma and pungency of flavour to Gewurztraminer. The less good examples can be overpowering and lacking in finesse.

Viognier is something of a curiosity in that it has long been used as an aromatic addition to the great red wines of Côte Rôtie, being vinified alongside the red grape Syrah and comprising up to 20 per cent of the final blend.

Viognier is being seen more often in Italy and Australia as well as in other parts of France, such as Languedoc-Roussillon, where some notable single varietals are being made and marketed under the name of the variety rather than the wines' geographic location. It has also gained popularity in California.

The grape has become hugely popular, with producers having to question whether or not investing in a potential money-spinner is worth the drawbacks of the grape's low productivity and its susceptibility to disease.

grüner veltliner

Grüner Veltliner has become hugely popular recently. It is particularly valued as a very successful food wine, combining the lusciousness of Pinot Gris, the bouquet of Riesling and the acidity of Sauvignon Blanc. It is being planted increasingly widely as its reputation spreads, in California, for example, Argentina and even China, although its heartland remains firmly in Austria, where it accounts for around 50% of the vineyard area (compared to barely 2% a couple of generations ago). The finest examples of all come from around the town of Krems, in Lower Austria, where it is capable of exhibiting a wonderful minerality and spicy acidity. But, given that Austria's entire wine production is barely half that of Bordeaux, they are going to have to continue to increase production if Grüner Veltliner is to become the next Viognier.

French country wines made from Colombard are ideal for knocking back, well chilled, at picnics or outdoors on late summer evenings.

Colombard originated in the Charente region of France and used to be distilled to make Cognac and Armagnac. It has been largely supplanted in this role by Ugni Blanc, as Trebbiano is known there, and so growers have turned to making it into simple, undemanding wines such as Vin de Pays des Côtes de Gascogne – crisp and spicy off-dry wines of high acidity and flowery perfume.

Remarkably, this productive but little-known grape is now one of the most widely planted varieties in California where – called French Colombard – it is prized for its ability to make simple crisp wines in a warm climate. For similar reasons it is also widely grown in both Australia and South Africa, where it is often blended with Chenin Blanc to make everyday drinking wines or sparklers.

colombard

müller-thurgau

Müller-Thurgau is a hybrid variety created in 1882 by Dr Hermann Müller, from the Swiss canton of Thurgau, who, in crossing Riesling with Sylvaner, hoped to combine the quality of the former with the early-ripening capability of the latter.

At its best, its wines are light, fresh, fruity and fragrant; at worst, they are bland, characterless and utterly lacking in flavour.

Müller-Thurgau is the most planted variety in Germany, making the infamous bottled bubble-gum, Liebfraumilch. The grape ripens almost anywhere, producing huge amounts of extremely dull, medium-dry, and some sweet, wine. The grape has a tendency to be a bit mousy in Germany though, and makes cleaner and fresher wines in Italy's Alto Adige, Luxembourg and in England, where it is widely planted.

The grape was once the mainstay of New Zealand's wine industry, producers believing it to be the variety best suited to their climate. It probably makes better wine there than it does anywhere else, but, as the industry has grown and tastes have become more sophisticated, so Chardonnay and Sauvignon Blanc have far outstripped Müller-Thurgau in terms of popularity.

Müller-Thurgau should be drunk on its own or with light, delicately flavoured dishes.

muscat

Muscat is thought to be the oldest variety known to man, its hundreds of different incarnations producing many styles of wine.

It may sound odd, but Muscat is the only grape to produce wine that actually tastes and smells of grapes.

One of the grape's best-known strains, Muscat Blanc à Petits Grains, is responsible for the fortified Muscat de Beaumes-de-Venise from the southern Rhône, and, blended with Clairette, the sparkling Clairette de Die in the northern Rhône.

In Greece, Muscat makes the dessert wines of Samos, Pátras and Cephalonia. In Italy, it is the flavour behind Asti Spumante. In Australia, known as Brown Muscat or Frontignan, it makes delicious fortified liqueur wines, as it does in California, where it is known as Muscat Blanc, Muscat Canelli or Muscat Frontignan.

Muscat Ottonel is grown in Alsace for heady dry wines and in Austria for sublime dessert wines. Muscat of Alexandria is usually used for table grapes, but in Spain it is used to make the heavy, sweet fortified wine Moscatel de Málaga and, in Portugal, Moscatel de Setúbal. Orange Muscat and Muscat Hamburg are grown in Australia and California for dessert wine; the latter, known as Black Muscat, is only rarely used.

sylvaner

Sylvaner originated in Austria, where it still thrives, albeit less ubiquitously than it once did. Despite being edged out by its own ungrateful offspring – Müller-Thurgau – as the country's most planted variety, Sylvaner is still much grown in Germany, mainly in Franken, Rheinhessen and Rheinpfalz. In Franken, where Riesling is difficult to ripen, it does especially well.

In France, Sylvaner is virtually unknown outside Alsace, where it makes easy-drinking, rather nondescript wines at the lower end of the price range. Even there, it is planted much less frequently than before. Switzerland remains true to the variety, especially in Valais where it is known as Johannisberg, making quaffable, refreshing wines of no great character. It used to be grown fairly widely in California, but in the charge to plant Sauvignon Blanc and Chardonnay it has all but been forgotten.

Sylvaner from Alsace goes well with onion tarts and quiches and is delicious with bouillabaisse.

A fritto misto eaten on the quayside of an Italian fishing village, washed downwith an Orvieto or Frascati, is hard to beat.

trebbiano

No grape produces more of the world's wine than Trebbiano, and it remains the most widely planted variety in France, where it is known as Ugni Blanc. The grape is notorious for producing bland, nondescript wines of little character, and so, on the principle that the worse the base wine the better the brandy, much of it is used for distillation.

In Italy it appears blended with other varieties in such wines as Frascati, Orvieto, Verdicchio, Soave, Vernaccia di San Gimignano and Est! Est!! Est!!!; it even finds its way into red Chianti.

Trebbiano is also grown in California – mainly in the San Joaquin Valley – and in Mexico, in both cases chiefly being used for distillation.

champagne and
sparkling wines

Briefly, champagne is made by adding yeast and sugar to previously blended Chardonnay, Pinot Meunier and Pinot Noir to encourage a second fermentation to occur in the bottle. To be called champagne, the wine may be made only by this method with these grapes in the region of Champagne in northern France. The sparkling wine that results is generally dry and white, although sweet champagnes, rosé champagnes and champagnes made solely from Chardonnay (known as *Blanc de Blancs*) or solely from a combination of Pinot Noir and Pinot Meunier (known as *Blanc de Noirs*) can also be found.

Most production is devoted to non-vintage (NV) champagne; wines from different vintages are

It is worth bearing in mind that the finest sparkling wines are often better – and are invariably cheaper – than the poorest champagnes.

blended to ensure consistency in each producer's distinctive house style. Rarer, vintage champagne is the wine of one outstanding year only. Still wines are also made in Champagne but are not often seen outside the region. 'Extra Brut' is the driest category of sparkling champagne, followed by 'Brut', both of which, confusingly, are drier even than 'Extra Dry' or 'Extra Sec'; 'Sec' is still less dry, 'Demi-Sec' is noticeably sweet, while 'Doux' is the sweetest of all.

Sparkling wines are made all over the world using the champagne method, with Germany, New Zealand, California, the Loire, Spain, Italy, South Africa and Australia all producing very good ones, usually from Chardonnay and Pinot Noir, although other grapes such as Chenin Blanc, Riesling and Aligoté are also used. Producers of such wines will label them *méthode traditionelle* to distinguish them from lesser wines made by cheaper methods.

dessert wines

The world's most celebrated dessert wines come from Sauternes and Barsac in Bordeaux, and from Germany and Hungary, although fine examples are also produced in Alsace, Austria, Australia, California, Canada and Greece.

A dessert wine can be sweet for a number of reasons: it might be a 'late-picked' wine, known in France as *vendange tardive*, made from extremely ripe grapes picked late in the season when their sweetness is most concentrated, or it might be a *vin doux naturel* such as Muscat de Beaumes-de-Venise, whose fermentation has been stopped by the addition of brandy before all the sugar has turned to alcohol.

Alternatively, like a Sauternes or Barsac, it might have been made from grapes affected by noble rot, the name given to *botrytis cinerea* – known as *pourriture noble* in France and *edelfäule* in Germany. Botrytis is a mould which, in areas prone to damp, humid conditions, attacks certain grapes, making them shrivel and rot, thereby concentrating their flavour and their sugars. Sauvignon Blanc, Sémillon, Gewurztraminer and Chenin Blanc in France and Riesling in Germany are particularly susceptible to this, and, the grapes having been picked individually by hand, produce dessert wines high in alcohol and richness of flavour. It is a laborious and wasteful process, however, for while a single vine is capable of producing a bottle of ordinary wine, it will produce only one glass of Sauternes.

Puddings are often greatly improved by an accompanying glass of dessert wine – a German Trockenbeerenauslese, perhaps, or a sweet Vouvray. But beware: some fruits can make such wines taste less sweet than usual and chocolate in particular is a tricky partner for wine, having a tendency to overwhelm even the greatest of dessert wines. But don't feel you have to keep the Sauternes, Barsac or Muscat de Beaumes-de-Venise for the pudding. Do as the French do and drink dessert wines well chilled with rich hors d'oeuvres such pâté de foie.

sherry

There are **several varieties** of sherry to suit all manner of tastes, which can be drunk on many **different occasions**.

Sherry comes from the deep south-west corner of Spain and takes its name from the town of Jerez de la Frontera. It is a fortified white wine made from Moscatel, Palomino and Pedro Ximénez, which is fermented in barrels above ground (rather than in cellars), and upon the surface of which a filmy growth called 'flor' grows, from which the wine gets its unique flavour.

The barrels of fermented and fortified wine are categorized by each wine's ageing potential. The new wine is added to a line of anything up to 100 butts, known as the *solera*. This is part of a process that involves the topping-up of older barrels with younger wine of the same style so that the wine is continuously being blended, ensuring that it always tastes the same – while mature wine ready for blending comes out of the other end.

Although the wines are usually sold under brand names such as Tio Pepe (from Gonzalez Byass) or La Ina (from Domecq), the label will also state what style of sherry it is.

Manzanilla, the appetizingly tangy sherry that comes from Jerez's neighbouring town of Sanlúcar de Barrameda, and Fino are the driest sherries. Their zip and freshness make both these sherries wonderful kick-starters for the appetite. Amontillado is effectively an aged Fino, whose time spent in the cask imparts a medium-dry nuttiness to the flavour .

Cream sherry is the sweetest, but it tends to lack the richness and fullness of flavour to be found in a top-class Oloroso, which, although packed with concentrated fruit aromas, can be dry or sweet to the taste.

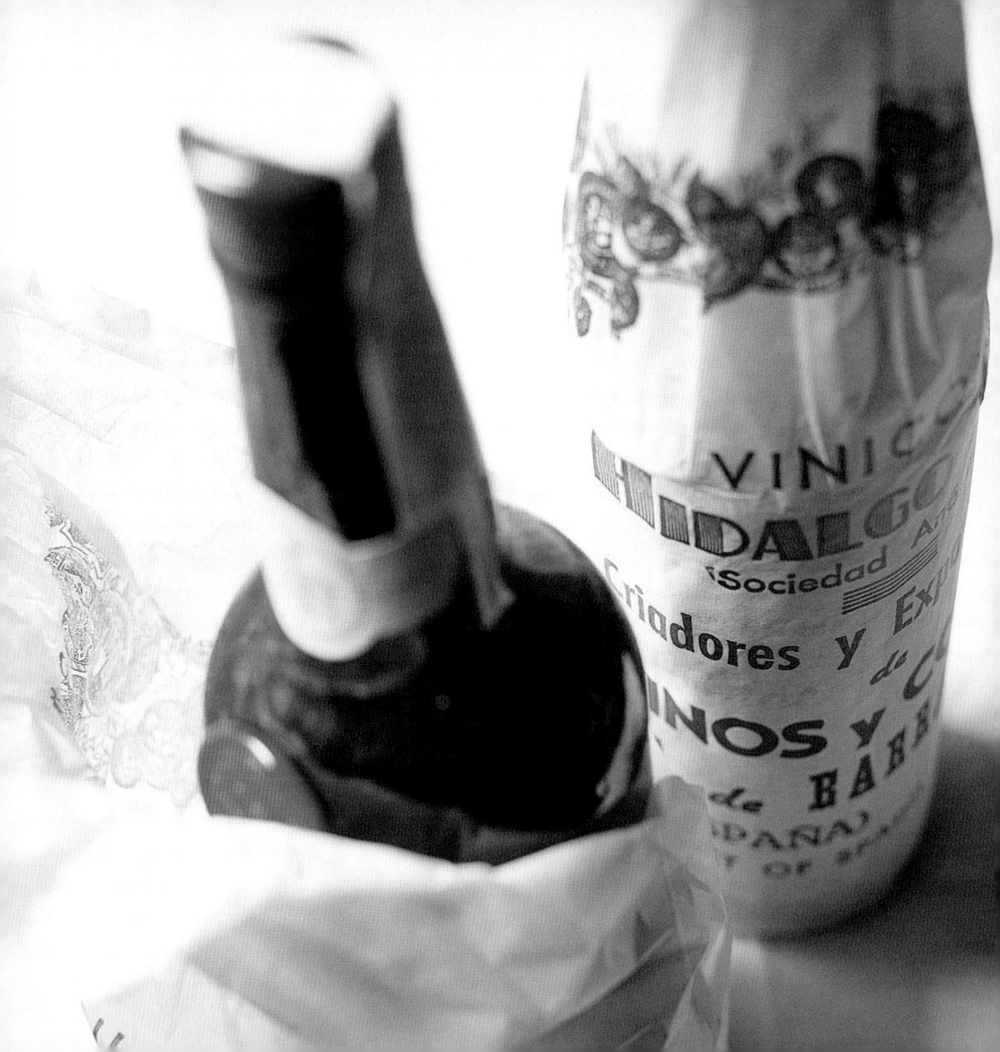
HIDALGO
Sociedad
Criadores y
de

vintages

Differences between wines are caused by the grapes, the soil in which they were grown, the way in which the wines were made and, above all, by the weather. In the wine-producing parts of California and Australia, blessed with relatively constant temperatures and clement weather, variations between years are less pronounced than they are in Europe, where a late frost, a hail storm or lack of sunshine can mean the difference between success and failure for a harvest.

If a blend of two or more vintages is used, the resultant wine will be known as non-vintage or NV, and will show no date on the label.

Except in the case of fine wines, the listing of a vintage date on a bottle of wine should not be taken as a guarantee of quality but rather as simply a matter of record and a note of the wine's age.

Recent fine vintages for white burgundy include 1990, 1992, 1995, 1996, 1997, 2000, 2001, 2002, 2004, 2005, 2006.

Among recent fine vintages for Sauternes are 1988, 1989, 1990, 1996, 1997, 2001, 2005, 2007.

Vintage champagne (like vintage port) is made only in exceptional years, the best of late being 1990, 1995, 1996, 1998, 2002, 2003, 2004.

a g e i n g

Ageing is the process by which wines settle down after fermentation, mature and improve, and nowhere do they do this better than in oak barrels.

Great differences are achieved by the size of the barrel, the type of oak used (usually *Limousin* or *Tronçais*) and by whether it is old oak or new oak, or a mixture of the two. New oak contains vanillin, which leads wines that have been in oak for any length of time to smell of vanilla. Chardonnay is particularly well suited to spending time in oak, by which process it takes on a deeper colour and fuller, softer, vanilla-like flavours. Indeed, it is extraordinary how much flavour Chardonnay does get from oak.

Some producers prefer not to use oak, because they feel that it imparts too much flavour to their wines, and so use stainless steel instead. Other producers feel that oak is essential whilst some even use oak chips as a rather unsatisfactory short cut method to imparting the unique flavour associated with oak.

laying down

While many red wines benefit from being kept for several years, allowing the tannins to soften and the fruit to develop with the passage of time, there are only a few white wines that gain from being laid down. This is partly because most white wine that is available from an off-licence or a supermarket is ready to drink there and then, and will not improve or increase in value, and partly because the majority of white wines do not need long to mature.

White burgundies, Chablis, white Rhônes, German and Alsace wines, the dessert wines of Sauternes and Barsac and vintage champagnes are all worth laying down for a few years provided that they are of middling to top quality and that they are from fine years. As they age, such wines will develop deeper colours and complex toasty and nutty flavours, along with rich honey tones in the case of the dessert wines. With luck, they might also increase in value.

wine in restaurants

A good restaurant should pride itself on having top-quality house wines, and you should feel confident about ordering them. When the bottle arrives, check that it is exactly what you ordered (vintage, château, etc.). You should also make sure that it is opened at the table, and check that its temperature is satisfactory. If the white is too warm, ask for it to be put in an ice bucket.

Unless you have ordered house wine, it is likely that you will be asked to taste the wine. There is no need to feel awkward. Relax: almost everything that could possibly be wrong with the wine can be discovered by looking at it in the glass and by smelling it. It should look bright and clear and, in the rare event of something being wrong with it, will smell mouldy, stale or tainted. It is hard to think of any wine – other than, perhaps, white Rhône, which can often smell like sherry – that doesn't flutter its eyelids at you. Many restaurants now sell wine by the glass – especially useful if you fancy a slurp of dessert wine with pudding.

A good restaurant should pride itself on having top-quality house wines, and you should feel confident about ordering them.

food and wine

When matching wine with food, the only rule is don't be afraid to experiment. Trial and error is the only way to find that perfect pairing where wine and food combine in harmony, each enhancing the other.

Generally speaking, the lighter the dish, the lighter the wine should be, and the heavier the dish, the heavier the wine, but everyone's taste differs. While you should bear in mind the experience of those who have trodden this path before you, the only way to find out what you like is to try it for yourself. The pairings listed below should be considered as no more than suggestions and ideas to set you on your way. Wine was created to accompany food, and you will be surprised at some of the unlikely pairings that succeed. Be brave and enjoy!

Aperitifs Champagne or sparkling wine, if the occasion demands it, or, alternatively, a well-chilled Fino or Manzanilla will kick-start the most jaded of appetites.

Beef
BEEF STEWS AND CASSEROLES A big, oak-aged Chardonnay from Burgundy or Australia.
ROAST BEEF Red might be the obvious choice, but a Pinot Gris from Alsace has the weight and the depth of flavour to make a very decent substitute.
Biscuits An Amontillado sherry or a medium-dry Vouvray.
Brunch Champagne or sparkling wine if your stomach can cope, a Bloody Mary if it can't (remember that a perfect Bloody Mary has a dash of Amontillado sherry added to it).
Canapés Sparkling wine, chilled Fino or Manzanilla sherry or any light, dry white wine.
Cheese
BLUE CHEESES (such as Stilton, Dolcelatte, Gorgonzola) An intensely sweet Sauternes or Beerenauslese cannot be bettered.
CHEESE ON TOAST A dry white Bordeaux or Rhône.
GOATS' CHEESE Try a bone-dry white wine or an intensely sweet one instead of the more usual red.

SOFT CHEESES (such as Brie and Camembert) Surprisingly, an unoaked Chardonnay from Chablis, say, or New Zealand, often makes a better partner than a red wine to soft cheeses.
STRONG CHEESES (such as Münster or Roquefort) A late-harvest Gewurztraminer from Alsace or an Icewine from Canada – both served well chilled – will make you wonder why you have never tried such a pairing before.
Chicken
CHICKEN IN CREAMY SAUCES Such dishes need a wine with character, such as an Alsace Pinot Gris or a New Zealand Sauvignon Blanc.
CHICKEN LIVER PÂTÉ A dry white from Burgundy or Bordeaux, or even a Viognier.
ROAST CHICKEN A full-flavoured white wine such as New World Chardonnay or mature white burgundy will hit the spot.
COLD CHICKEN Any white wine with a bit of oomph will do, such as a white Rhône or a white Rioja.
Chinese food see Takeaways.

Cold meats Ham and salami go especially well with full-flavoured wines such as Alsace Pinot Gris, California Chardonnay, Australian Semillon/Chardonnay and New Zealand Sauvignon Blanc.

Curry *see* Takeaways.

Duck

ROAST DUCK An aromatic Viognier or a top-quality Chablis or Alsace is needed.

Egg dishes Eggs aren't the ideal partners for wine, but a plate of scrambled eggs and smoked salmon always seems to demand champagne or top-quality sparkling wine.

Fish

GRILLED SOLE OR PLAICE Such a simple dish will allow any top-quality wine to show off, such as the best white burgundy or Chablis you can lay your hands on.

GRILLED TURBOT AND TUNA A white Rhône or Rioja works well.

GRILLED PRAWNS Any dry white wine will do.

GRILLED OR POACHED SALMON Chablis, white burgundy or New World Chardonnay.

FISH PIE Try a Sauvignon Blanc from New Zealand or Chile.

FISH IN CREAMY SAUCES Such dishes are well-partnered by Riesling from Alsace or Germany.

BOUILLABAISSE Any dry wine from the Loire – a Pouilly Fumé or Sancerre if you are in funds, a Muscadet or Sauvignon de Touraine if you are not.

FISH AND CHIPS *see* Takeaways.

FISH PÂTÉ An aromatic Viognier or an Alsace Riesling would be perfect.

FRITTO MISTO A light, dry Italian such as Orvieto or Frascati.

SMOKED EEL, MACKEREL AND SALMON Australian Semillon or Alsace Gewurztraminer.

SMOKED HADDOCK OR COD White Rhône or full-bodied Chardonnay.

GRAVADLAX Chablis, New World Chardonnay or Viognier.

GRILLED TROUT Try an English wine – oh, go on!

Foie gras Top-quality sweet wine such as Sauternes or a dry Viognier.

Fruit *see* Puddings.

Goose Something big and highly flavoured is needed, such as an Alsace Pinot Gris or an Hermitage Blanc. You might even consider an off-dry

Riesling such as a German Spätlese.

Greek food Retsina is the obvious choice for the taramasalata and calamari, but as Retsina is something of an acquired taste you might prefer a Muscadet or an Italian Chardonnay.

Ham *see* Cold cuts.

Indian food *see* Takeaways.

Lamb

ROAST LAMB Something full-flavoured but dry is needed if you are eschewing red wine, an Hermitage Blanc perhaps.

Mexican food Sauvignon Blancs from Chile, California or New Zealand probably work best.

North African food It is best to stick to full-bodied wines from the Rhône or the New World.

Nuts You won't go wrong with a Fino or Manzanilla sherry.

Olives Dry sherry works best of all.

Onion tart *see* Quiche.

Pacific Rim Riesling works best with this style of cooking, as does almost anything from Alsace.

Pasta

WITH SEAFOOD SAUCE Almost any white wine from Italy, such as Orvieto, Frascati, Soave and Verdicchio.

WITH PESTO SAUCE Ditto, although a simple unoaked Chardonnay works well too.

Picnics A well-chilled French country wine such as a Côtes de Gascogne if there are lots of you, but treat yourselves to vintage champagne if there are only two of you.

Pork

ROAST PORK Any full-bodied white wine will do.

LOIN OF PORK Australian Semillon works well.

Prosciutto with melon Try an Italian white such as Orvieto, Frascati or Verdicchio.

Puddings

CAKE Oloroso or cream sherry.

CHOCOLATE PUDDINGS The only wines that can really stand up to chocolate are the Black Muscats and Orange Muscats of California and Australia.

CUSTARDS Sauternes or Monbazillac.

FRESH FRUIT Fruit can be tricky, so it is advisable to stick to a sweet Coteaux du Layon or Vouvray.

FRUIT TARTS German or Austrian Beerenauslese, or a late-harvest Alsace Gewurztraminer.

STRAWBERRIES AND CREAM A sweet Vouvray or a sweet sparkler like Asti Spumante.

ICE CREAM AND SORBETS On this occasion, take a break from the wine.

Quiche or Onion tart Any wine from Alsace.

Risotto Italian Pinot Grigio.

Salads Something dry and light such as a Muscadet and Chilean Sauvignon Blanc.

Seafood

CAVIAR If you are eating caviar, it probably means that someone else is paying, so insist on champagne.

DRESSED CRAB Dry German Riesling or white Rioja.

COLD LOBSTER White Rhône or Alsace Pinot Gris.

LOBSTER THERMIDOR This dish gives you the chance to retrieve from your cellar an old white burgundy, top-quality New World Chardonnay or Hermitage Blanc.

SAUTÉED SCALLOPS Dry German Riesling or New Zealand Sauvignon Blanc.

OYSTERS Sancerre, Pouilly Fumé or Black Velvet (champagne and draught Guinness, half and half, in a pint tankard).

MOULES ET FRITES Muscadet or Belgian beer.

Soup It depends on what sort of soup it is, but dry sherry usually works well.

Sushi and sashimi Sake (served hot) or full-flavoured New World Chardonnay.

Takeaways

CHINESE A medium-dry German Riesling or a California Chardonnay are fine.

INDIAN An ice-cold medium-dry Vouvray or an off-dry Orvieto, unless you are sticking to beer.

FISH AND CHIPS Champagne or any dry English wine.

THAI FOOD Spicy food typical of Thai cuisine needs a spicy Gewurztraminer.

TAPAS Sherry, of course (although any decent white wine will do).

Turkey

ROAST TURKEY Such a dreary dish as roast turkey needs a wine with plenty of character.

COLD TURKEY So does cold turkey – but even more so.

Veal

ROAST VEAL A big, oak-aged Chardonnay from Burgundy or Australia.

VEAL IN CREAM SAUCE Pouilly Fumé or Sancerre or even Alsace Riesling.

Vegetables

ROAST VEGETABLES An oaky Chardonnay from Australia or California is an idea partner for roast vegetables.

quality
classifications

Wine laws are very strict and their purpose is twofold: to protect the producer by ensuring that his region's reputation isn't undermined by the unscrupulous practices of some rogue producer, and to protect the consumer by guaranteeing the basic quality and character of the wine.

In general, France's stringent *Appellation d'Origine Contrôlée* (AOC) laws give a guarantee of a wine's origins and the authenticity of the grape variety, but without guaranteeing quality. The categories below AOC are *Vins Délimité de Qualité Supérieure* (VDQS), *Vin de Pays and Vin de Table*: these are for lower-quality wines and have less rigid production restrictions.

In Burgundy, a classification of *Premiers Crus* and *Grands Crus* identify the best vineyards, based on location; Alsace has elements of both systems.

Italy has a similar system, the *Denominazione di Origine Controllata* (DOC), although many top producers consider it too restrictive and make great wines which are obliged to be classified as Vino da Tavola. A new classification, *Indicazione Geografica Tipica* (IGT) has been introduced to alleviate some of the confusion.

Germany's classifications of quality refer to the ripeness of the grapes and therefore to the sweetness of the wine.

Virtually every European wine-growing region has its own rules about which grapes may be used where and by what method they may be grown and vinified. Where they do not exist, individual producers may create a structure of their own.

Spain and Italy designate their wines *Reserva* or *Riserva* to indicate a certain period in oak, a treatment that is usually confined to only the best wines, unlike the French, whose categories relate to location.

New World wines are not subject to such strict restrictions – something that is often more than made up for by producers' giving extraordinarily detailed information on the back label.

storing

serving

Only a few white wines improve with age – for example, top-class white burgundy, Chablis, Sauternes and vintage champagne. Most white wine is likely to be for immediate consumption.

Store white wines as you would red wines, on their sides somewhere cool and dark and away from damp, vibration and strong smells. Wooden wine racks are readily available and can be shaped to fit the most awkward spots. Alternatively, you can do a lot worse than use a cardboard wine box lying on its side.

White wine is best served chilled rather than ice cold; an hour in the fridge should be sufficient.

To open a champagne bottle, remove the foil and wire and hold the bottle at a slant with its base in your strong hand and the cork in the other hand. Hold the cork firmly while twisting the bottle slowly; don't shake it. Ease the cork out gently covering it with your palm while ensuring that a glass is nearby in case the wine should froth out. Serve in tall glasses to preserve the bubbles that the winemaker has striven so hard to achieve.

tasting

Fill no more than a quarter of your glass and look at the wine, preferably against a white background. The wine should be clear and bright without any cloudiness or haziness. Holding the stem, swirl the glass around to release the bouquet. Take a good sniff; it should smell clean and fresh. Almost anything that might be wrong with a wine can be detected on the nose – by odours of mustiness, perhaps, or dampness.

Take a mouthful of the wine, drawing air into the mouth as you do so. Roll the liquid around your tongue and then spit or swallow. What is it like? Is it sweet or dry, light or full-bodied? Does it remind you of anything? The taste of a fine wine remains in the mouth, and its many components – its acidity, alcohol, fruit and tannin – should have combined so pleasantly that you want nothing more than to take another sip.

glossary

Acid/acidity Acids occur naturally in wine and are crucial in giving it character and structure and in helping it to age.

Aroma The varietal smell of a wine.

Balance A wine's harmonious combination of acids, tannins, alcohol, fruit and flavour.

Bereich (German) Term for a wine-producing district.

Bianco (Italian) White.

Blanc (French) White.

Blanc de blancs (French) A white wine made only from white grapes.

Blanc de noirs (French) A white wine made only from black (red) grapes.

Blanco (Spanish) White.

Blind tasting A tasting of wines at which the labels and shapes of the bottles are concealed from the tasters.

Bodega (Spanish) Winery.

Body The weight and structure of a wine.

Botrytis cinerea A fungus that, when it shrivels and rots white grapes, concentrates their flavours and sugars, leading to dessert wines that are high in alcohol and richness of flavour.

It is also known as noble rot, *pourriture noble* and *edelfäule*.

Bouquet The complex scent of a wine that develops as it matures.

Cantina (Italian) Winery or cellar.

Cave (French) Cellar.

Cellar book A useful way to note what wines you have bought, from where and at what price, as well as recording when you consumed them and what they tasted like.

Cepa (Spanish) Term for vine variety.

Cépage (French) Term for vine variety.

Chai (French) Place for storing wine.

Château (French) Term for a wine-growing property – chiefly used in Bordeaux.

Clos (French) Enclosed vineyard.

Corkage Charge per bottle levied on those customers in restaurants who bring in their own wine to drink.

Corked Condition, indicated by a musty odour, where a wine has been contaminated by a faulty cork.

Cosecha (Spanish) Vintage.

Côte (French) Hillside of vineyards.

Crémant (French) Semi-sparkling.

Cru (French) Growth or vineyard.

Cuvée (French) A blended wine or a special selection.

Demi-sec (French) Semi-sweet.

Dolce (Italian) Sweet.

Domaine (French) Property or estate.

Doux (French) Sweet.

Dulce (Spanish) Sweet.

Fermentation The transformation of grape juice into wine, whereby yeasts – naturally present in grapes and occasionally added in cultured form – convert sugars into alcohol.

Frizzante (Italian) Semi-sparkling.

Grand cru (French) Term used for top-quality wines in Alsace, Bordeaux, Burgundy and Champagne.

Halbtrocken (German) Medium dry.

Horizontal tasting A tasting of several different wines that all come from the same vintage.

Jahrgang (German) Vintage.

Keller (German) Cellar.

Landwein (German) A level of quality wine just above simple table wine, equivalent to the French *vin de pays*.

Late harvest Very ripe grapes picked late when their sweetness is most concentrated.

Méthode traditionelle The method – involving a secondary fermentation in bottle – by which champagnes and top-quality sparkling wines are made.

Moelleux (French) Sweet.

Mousse (French) The effervescence that froths in a glass of sparkling wine when it is poured, and which seems to wink at you.

Mousseux (French) Sparkling.

Négoçiant (French) Wine merchant, shipper or grower who buys wine or grapes in bulk from several sources before vinifying and/or bottling the wine himself.

Non-vintage (NV) Term applied to a wine that is a blend of more than one vintage, notably champagne.

Nose The overall sense given off by a wine on being smelled. It is not just the wine's scent; the nose also conveys information about the wine's well-being.

Oak Much wine is aged in oak barrels, something which is typified by whiffs of vanilla or cedarwood.

Oxidized Term used to describe wine that has deteriorated owing to overlong exposure to air.

Perlant (French) A term that refers to a wine with the faintest of sparkles in it.

Perlwein (German) A type of low-grade semi-sparkling wine.

Pétillant (French) Slightly sparkling.

Phylloxera An aphid-like insect that attacks the roots of vines with disastrous results.

Récolte (French) Crop or vintage.

Sec (French) Dry.

Secco (Italian) Dry.

Seco (Spanish/Portuguese) Dry.

Sekt (German) The German, not for dry – which is *trocken* – but for sparkling wine.

Sommelier Wine waiter.

Spittoon Receptacle into which wine is expectorated at a wine tasting.

Spritzer A refreshing drink made from white wine and soda or sparkling mineral water and usually served with ice.

Spumante (Italian) Sparkling.

Sur lie Term given to the process of ageing wines on their lees or sediment prior to bottling, resulting in a greater depth of flavour.

Tafelwien (German) Table wine.

Trocken (German) Dry.

Varietal A wine named after the grape (or the major constituent grape) from which it is made.

Variety Term for each distinctive breed of grape.

Vendange (French) Harvest or vintage.

Vendange tardive (French) Late harvest.

Vendemmia (Italian) Harvest or vintage.

Vendimia (Spanish) Harvest or vintage.

Vertical tasting A tasting of several wines from the same property that all come from different vintages.

Vigneron (French) Wine grower.

Vin de pays (French) Country wine of a level higher than table wine.

Vin de table (French) Table wine.

Vin doux naturel (VDN) (French) A fortified wine that has been sweetened and strengthened by the addition of alcohol, either before or after fermentation.

Vin ordinaire (French) Basic wine not subject to any regulations.

Vinification Wine making.

Vino da tavola (Italian) Table wine.

Vino de mesa (Spanish) Table wine.

Vintage Both the year of the actual grape harvest as well as the wine made from those grapes.

Viticulture Cultivation of grapes.

index

acknowledgments

I would like to thank Anne Ryland for coming up with idea, and Alison Starling, Gabriella Le Grazie, Luis Peral-Aranda and Maddalena Bastianelli for making the project such an enjoyable one. I am also most grateful to Judith Murray, to David Roberts MW and to Alan Williams for his beautiful photographs, some of which were taken at Villandry and Berry Bros and Rudd Ltd, to whom also many thanks. Finally, of course, I would like to thank my wife Marina, ever patient and ever wise, and without whom . . .

Villandry
170 Great Portland Street
London W1N 5TB, UK
+ 44 (0)20 7631 3131
www.villandry.com

Berry Bros & Rudd Ltd
3 St James's Street
London SW1A 1EG, UK
+ 44 (0)870 900 4300
www.bbr.com

The author and publisher would also like to thank the following companies for allowing us to photograph their vineyards, wineries and cellars.

AUSTRALIA
Barossa Valley, South Australia
d'Arenberg, McLaren Vale,
South Australia
Rockford Vineyards, Barossa
Valley, South Australia

CALIFORNIA
Beringer Wine Estates, St Helena, Napa Valley
De Loach Vineyards, Sonoma Valley
Heitz Wine Cellars, St Helena, Napa Valley
Schramsberg Vineyards, Napa Valley